INSPIRED INNER GENIUS

David Attenborough

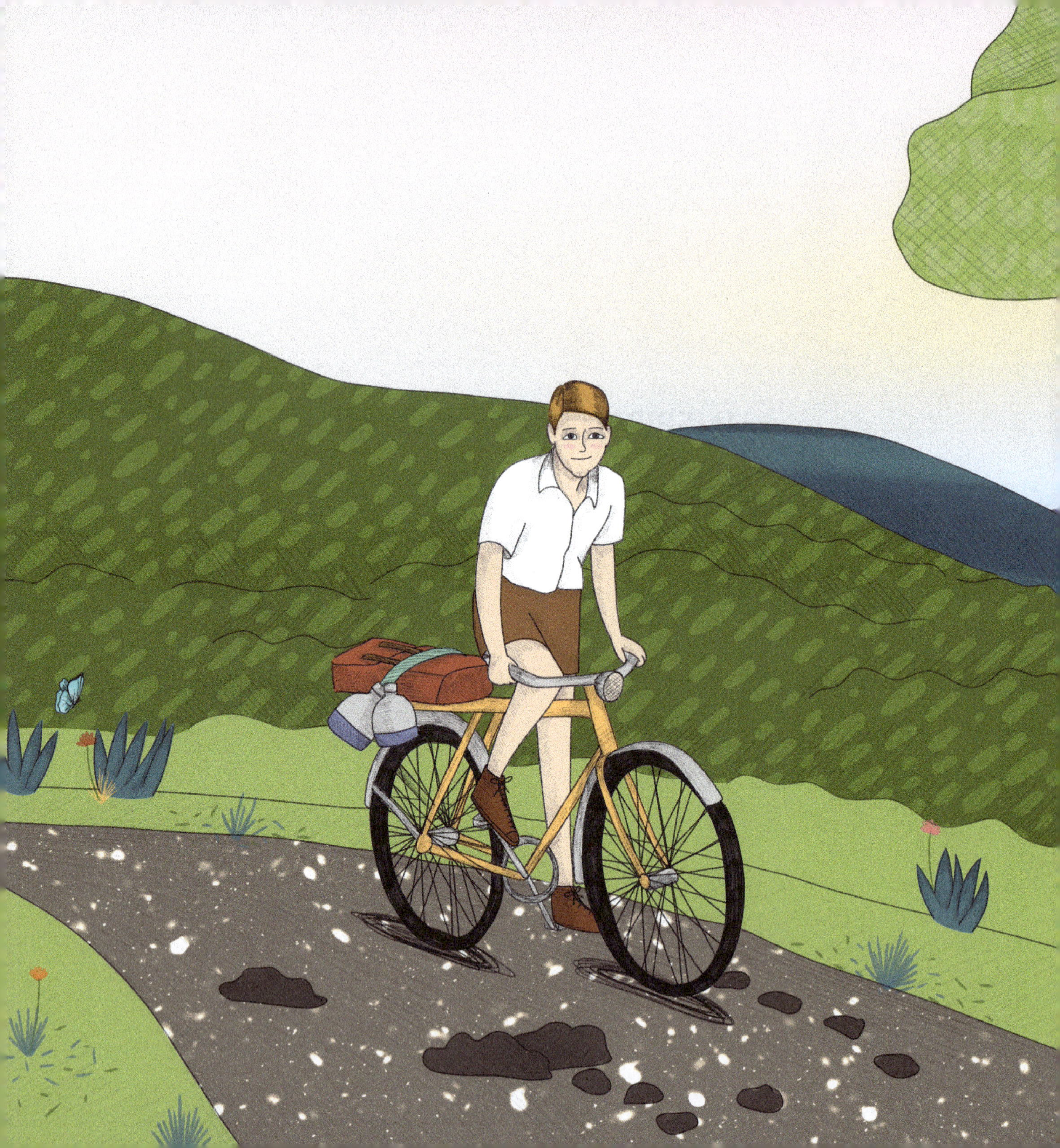

It's a hot day in the Lake District of England and a young boy rides his bicycle slowly along the road. He stops under a large tree and looks through his bag to find his canteen. As he pulls out his water, several rocks fall out...but these are no ordinary rocks, and this is no ordinary boy.

These rocks are really fossils[1] and this boy's name is David Attenborough. He picks up the fossils and places them back into his bag. He has been gone from home for almost three weeks. He hops back on his bike, unafraid of danger, hoping only to learn more about this big beautiful world!

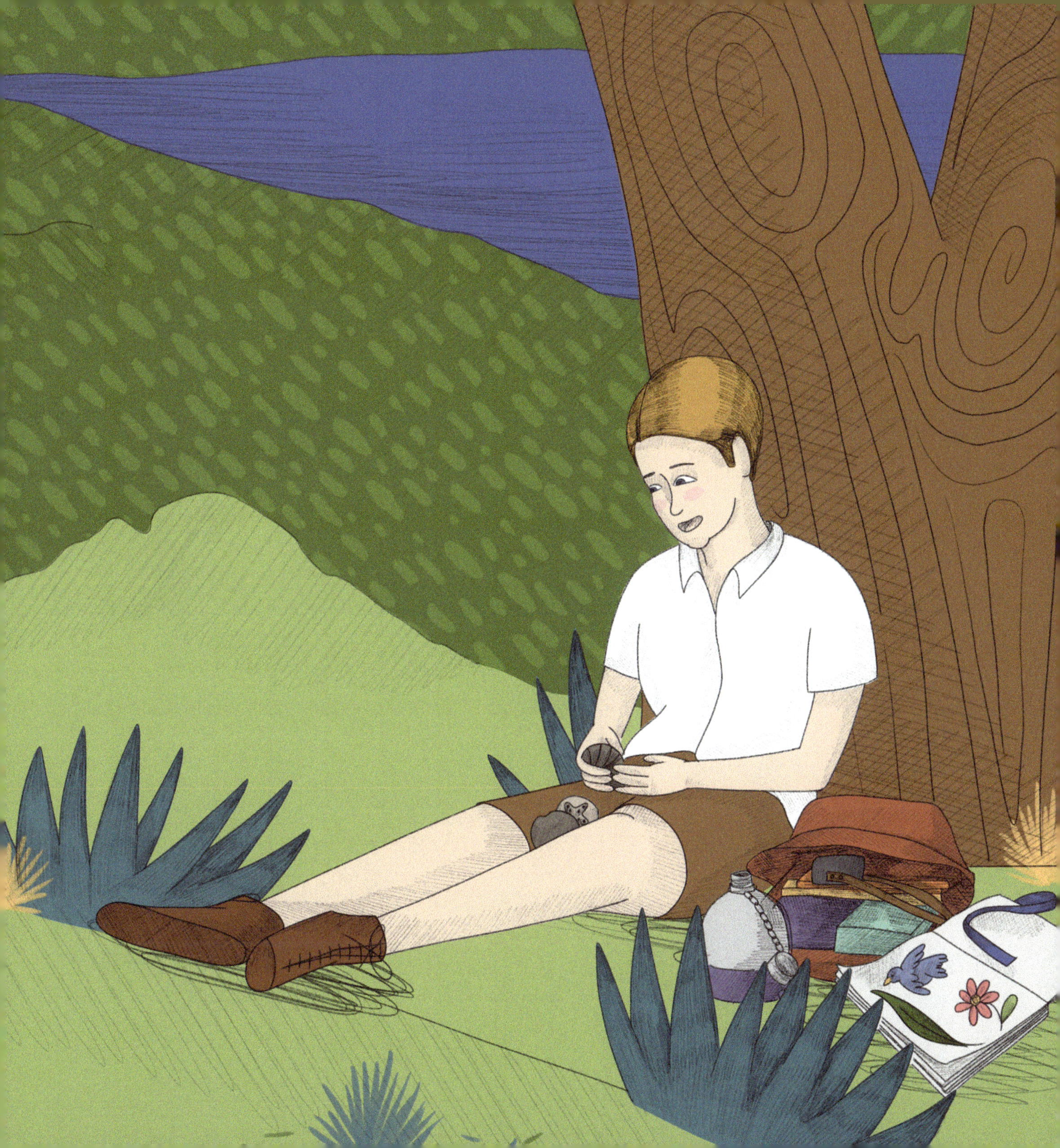

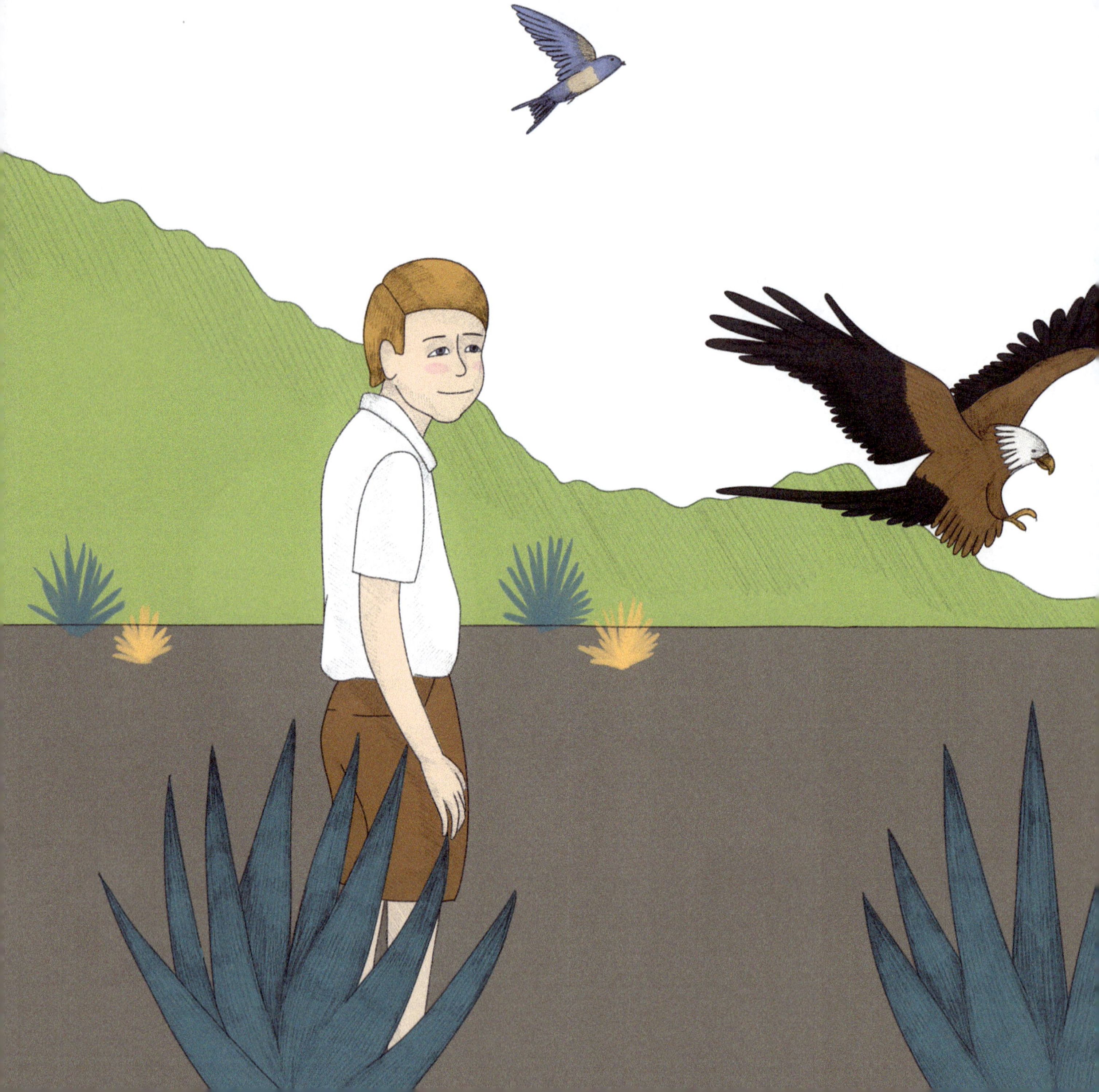

David was born the middle of 3 boys and grew up in Leicester, England. He always loved being in nature and was often found out in the fields, collecting fossils or bird's eggs. He studied natural sciences at the University of Cambridge. He began to work for the British Broadcasting Corporation and soon became a producer[2].

It might seem strange for someone who loved being outdoors to choose a career in television. But this is where David began to shine. Up to this point, there was little focus on educational programs, and certainly no shows about science. David wanted to change that.

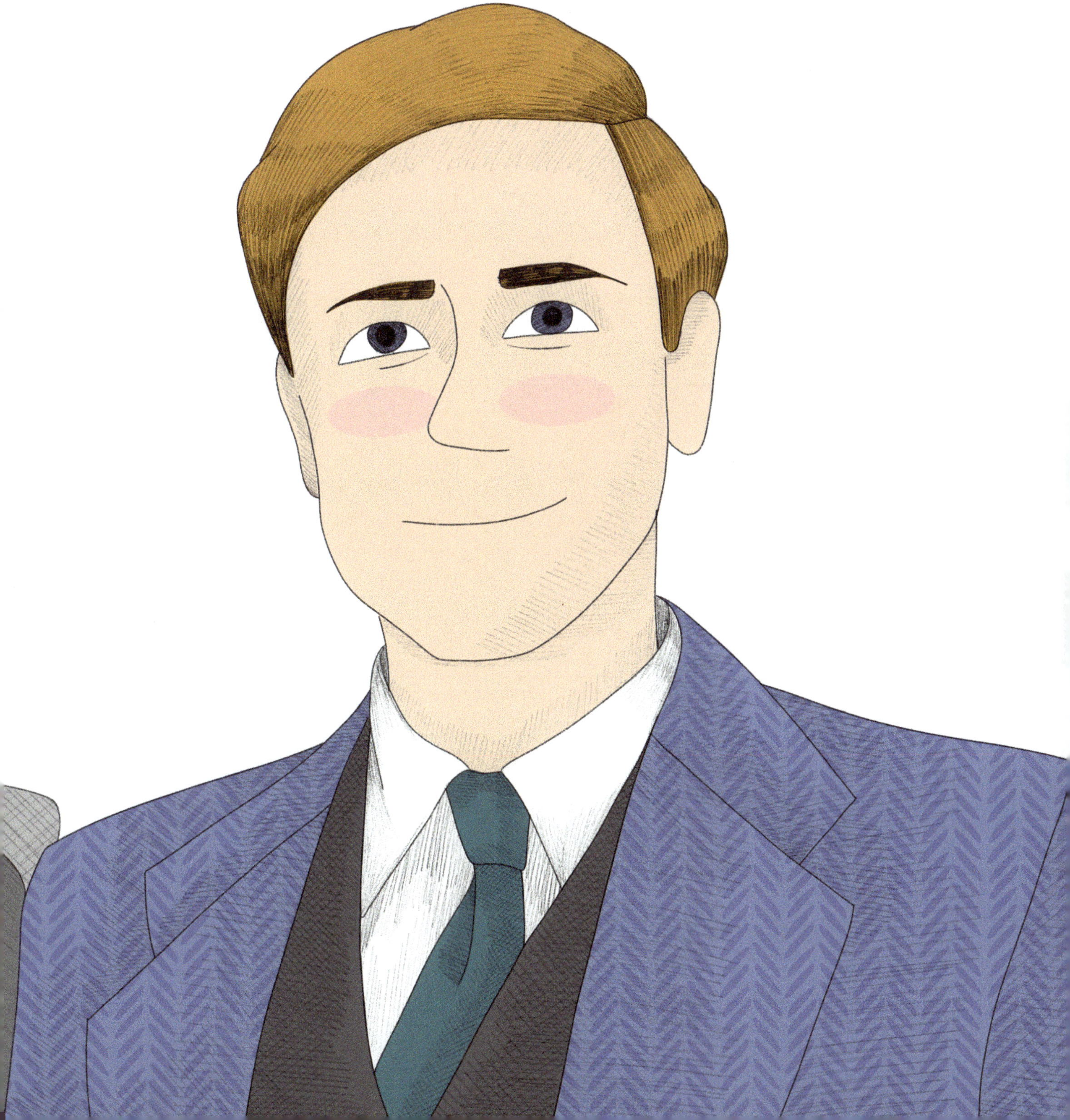

In 1954 he launched "Zoo Quest". Film crews learned to capture footage of animals in their natural habitat[3] without disturbing them. It was the first time a show like this had been made and it set the stage for more nature documentaries to follow.

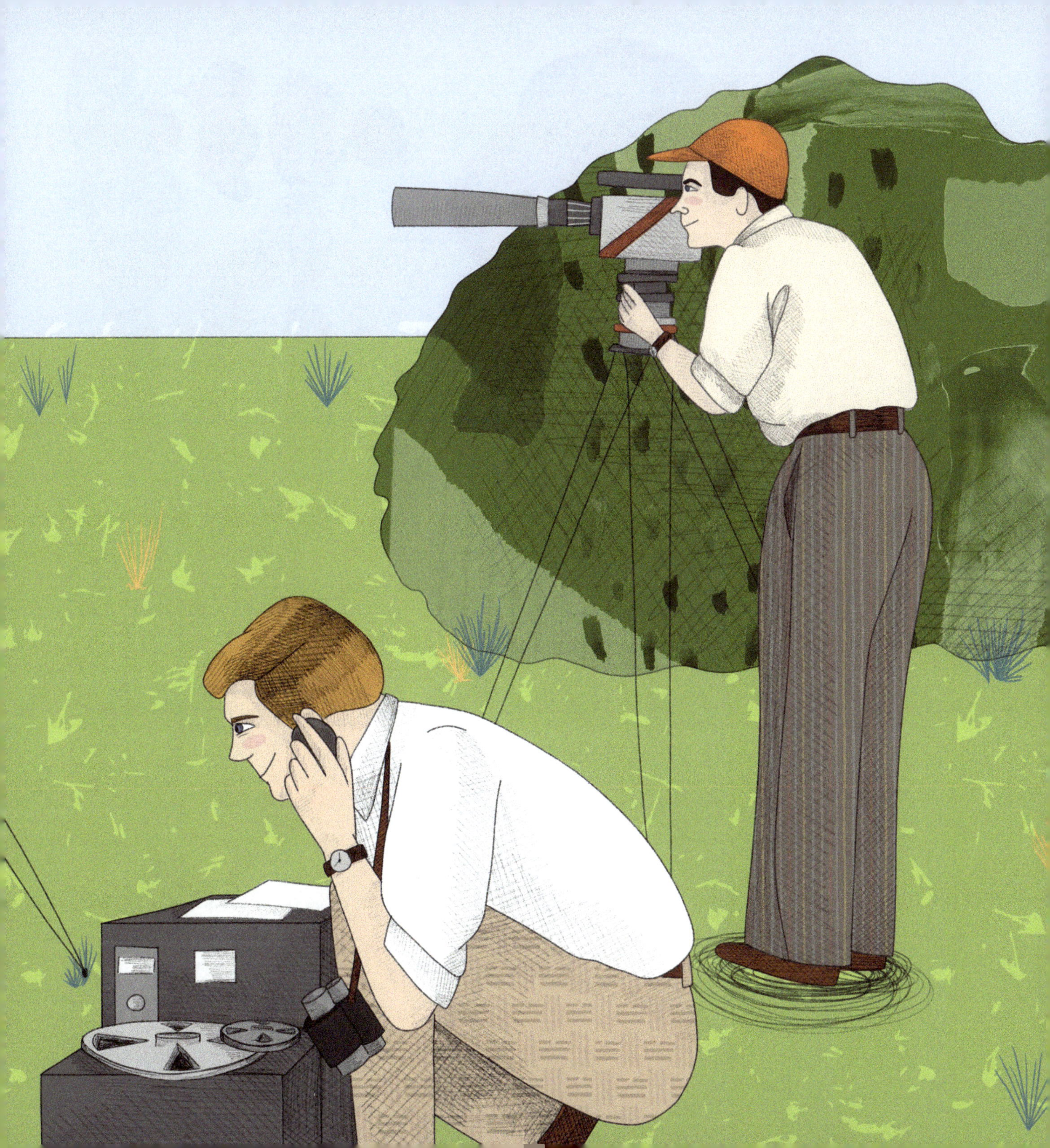

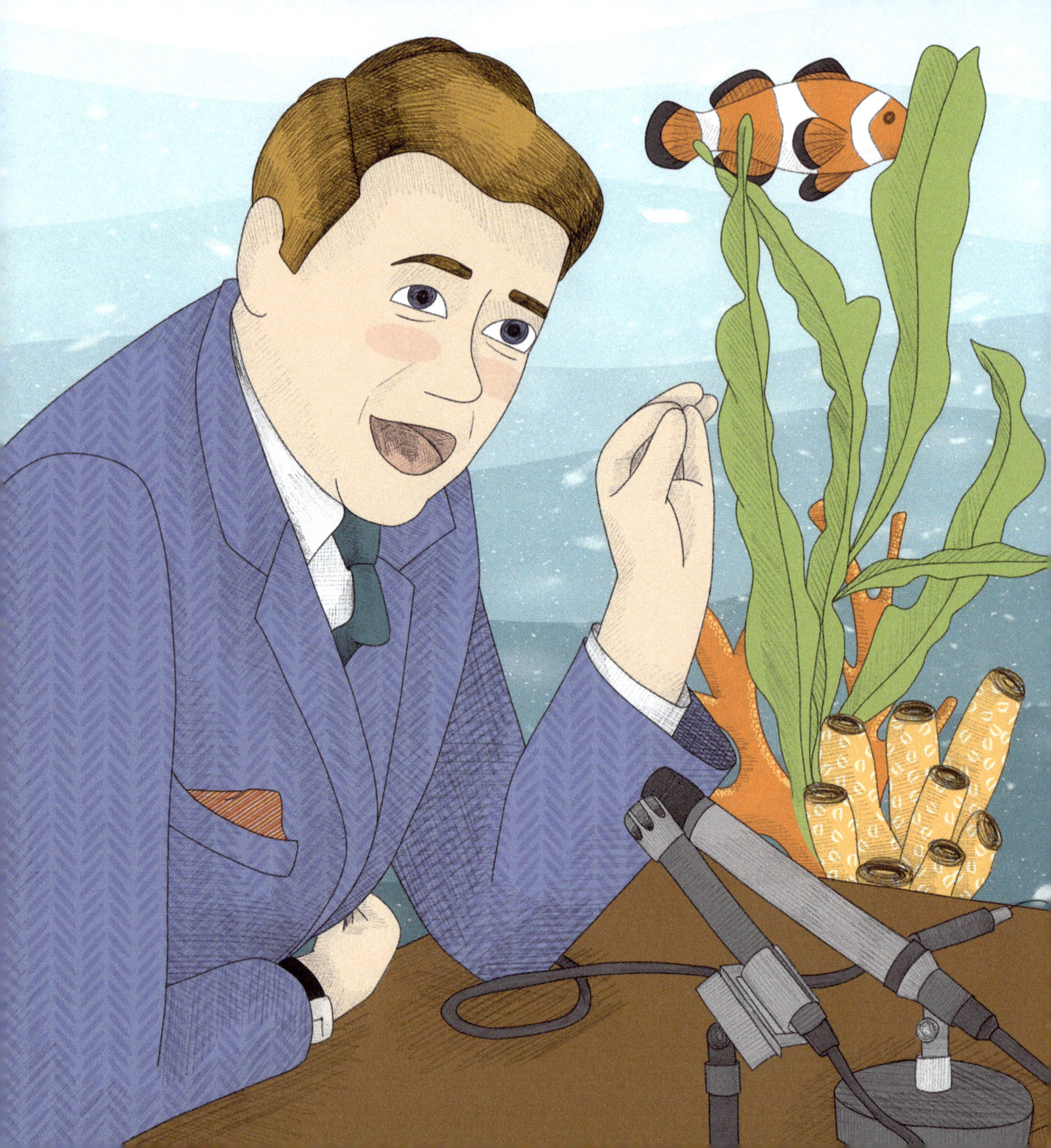

After working with the BBC for several years, David left to write and produce his own shows. The most famous program was called "Life on Earth". This show took film crews around the world, capturing footage of plants and animals. David's narration[4] brought these stories to life!

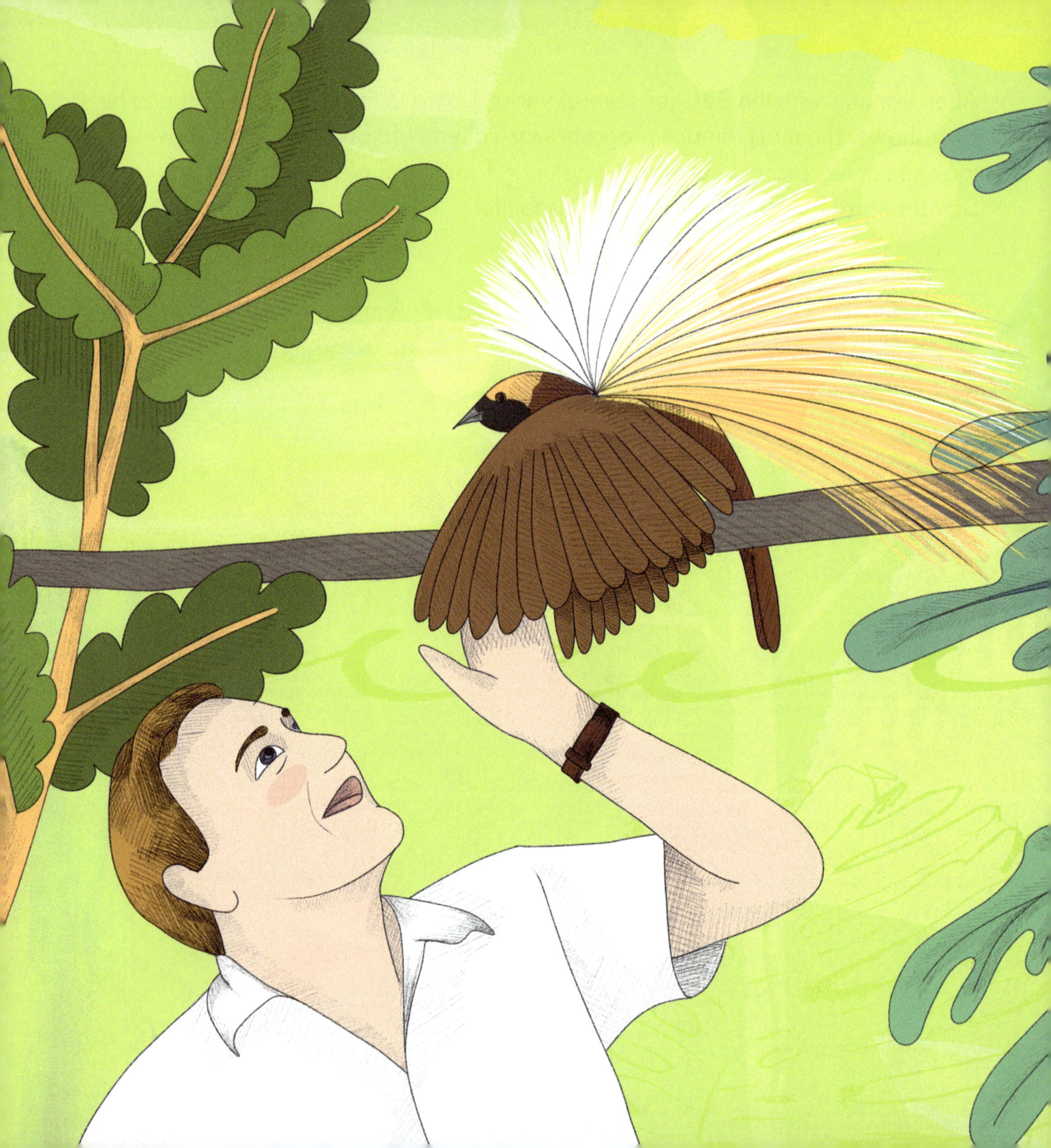

David produced and narrated dozens of shows. The "Life" series included shows about mammals, reptiles, birds, frozen landscapes, insects and more. "Blue Planet" featured oceans and marine life. "Attenborough in Paradise" was filmed in 1996 about his personal favorite animal: birds of paradise.

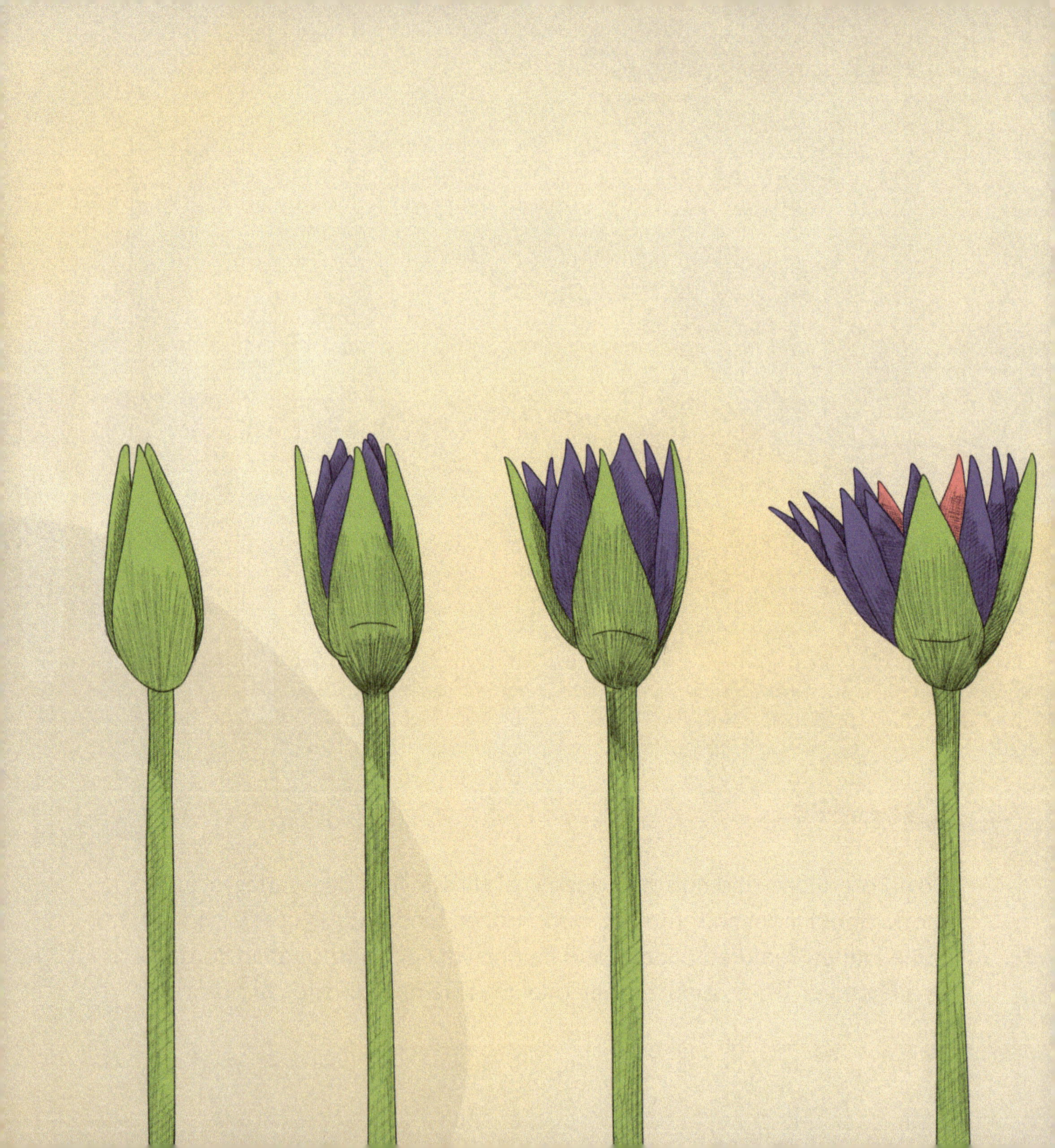

David found creative ways to use film techniques to tell a story. In the show "The Private Life of Plants" time-lapse[5] photography was used to show plants growing at a fast speed. Viewers got to see in a matter of minutes what might take hours, or even days, to happen in nature.

The shows he made were very successful. At one point, the wildlife series "Wildlife on One" had eight to ten million people watching it every week. All around the world people would tune in to learn more about the planet they lived on.

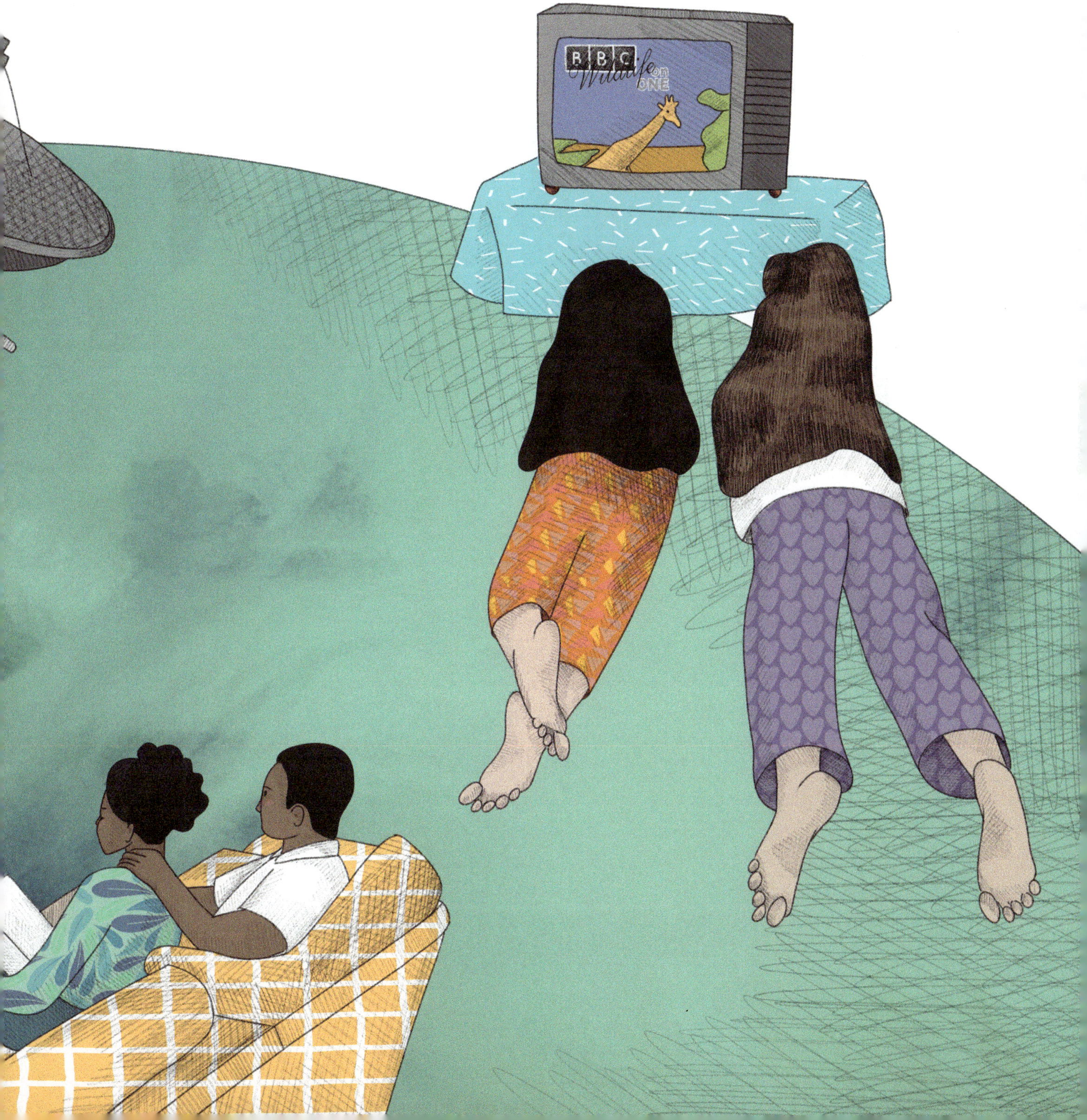
BBC
Wildlife on
ONE

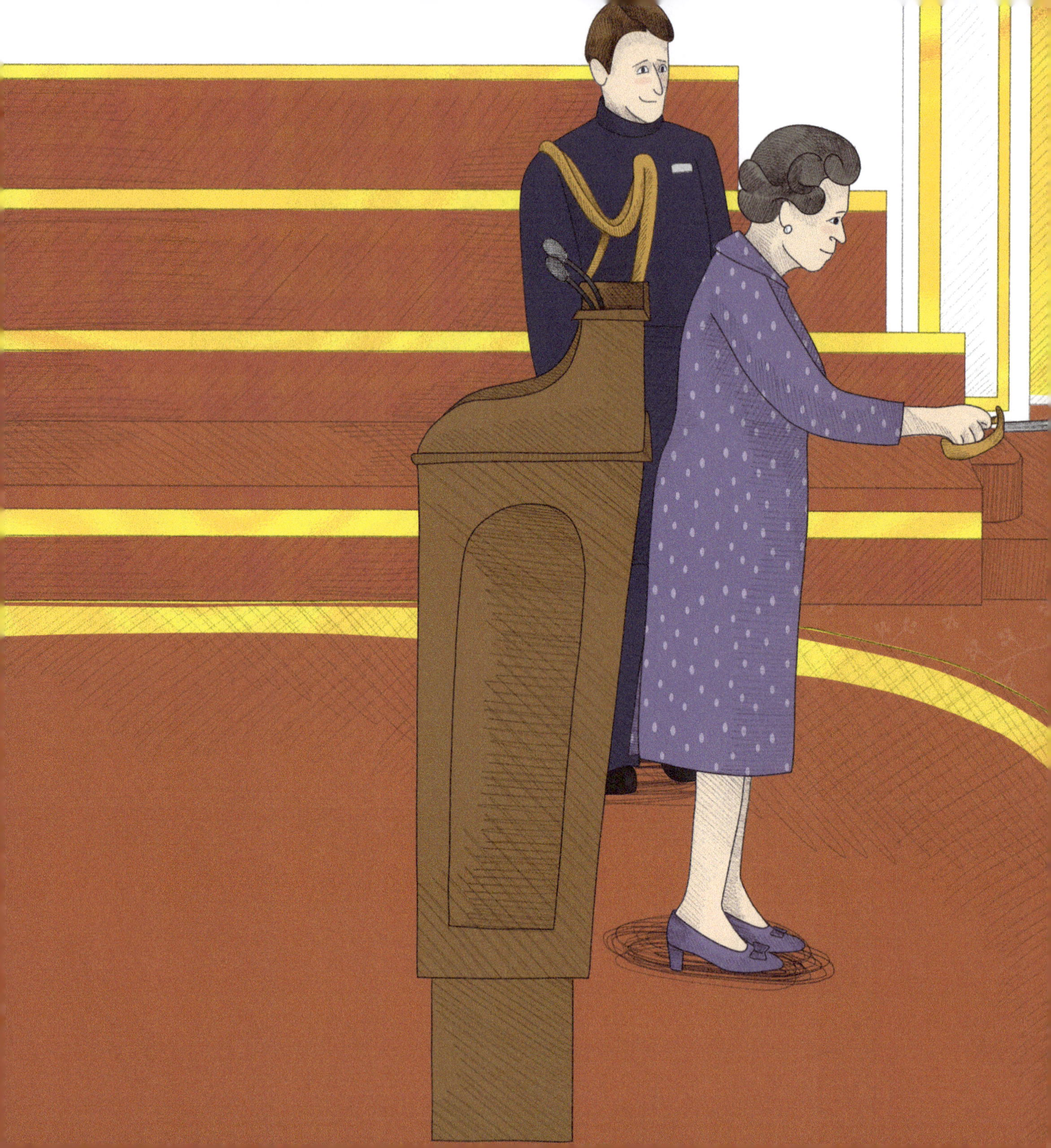

In 1985, he was knighted as Sir David Frederick Attenborough. He has also received many awards for the work he has done to educate people about the planet and the need to take care of it.

David has several animal species[6] named after him -- both living and extinct! A sea animal discovered to live millions of years ago is scientifically named "Attenborosaurus". And to honor his love of butterflies, a tropical butterfly found in Colombia and Brazil is named "Euptychia Attenboroughi".

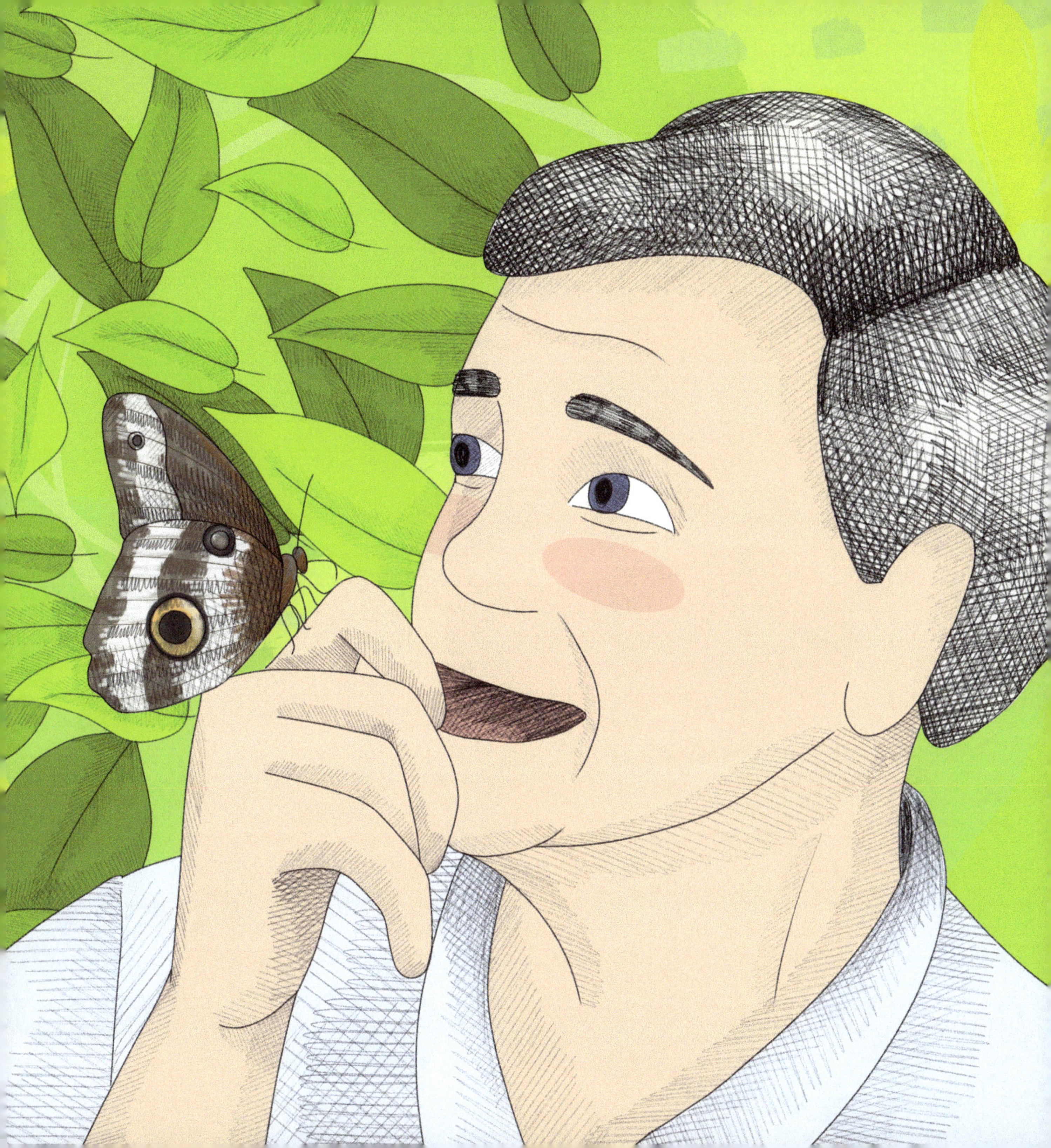

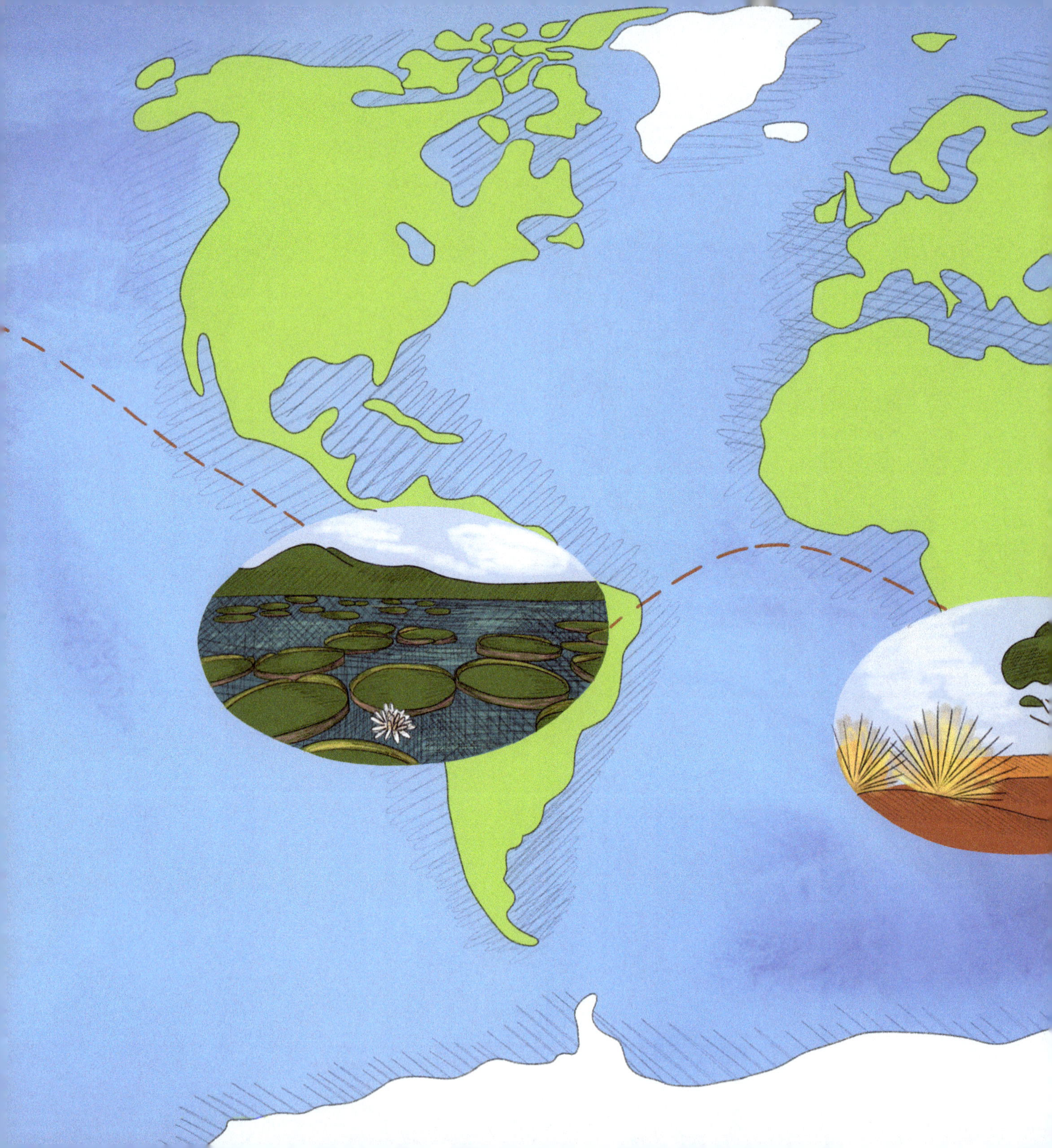

Just like when he was a boy riding his bike through the Lake District, David continues to explore the world, with no fear of danger. He keeps a full schedule[7] flying around the globe[8] to places like Australia, the Kalahari desert and the Borneo

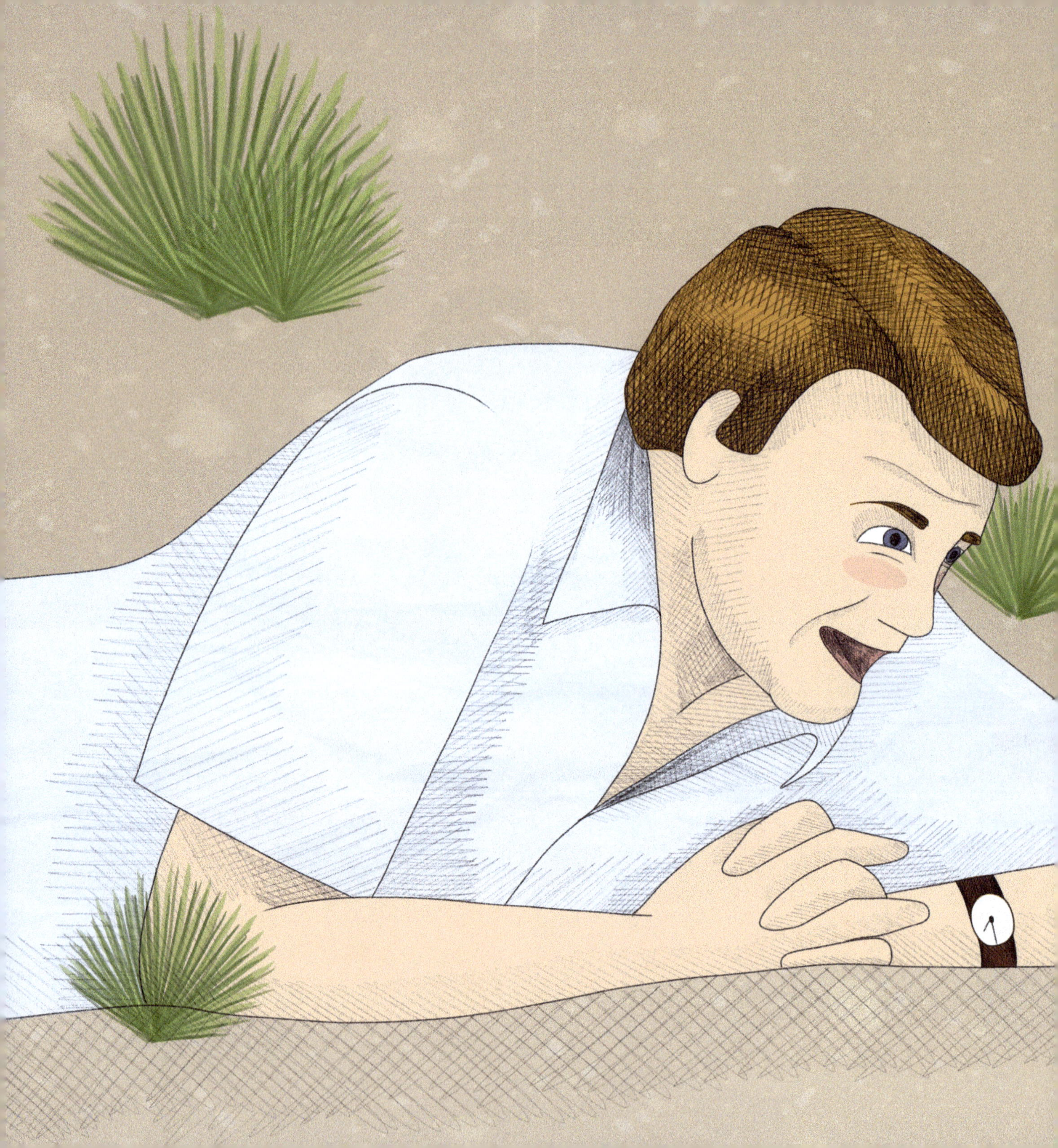

David's shows help people learn and care about the planet.
"No one will protect what they don't care about; and no one will care about what they have never experienced," he says. He opened up a world of beauty and science for people to see in their own living rooms!

GLOSSARY

1. Fossils — A piece of animal or plant from the past that has been preserved in the earth's crust; it is very hard like a rock.

2. Producer — The person in charge of making television shows.

3. Habitat — The place where a plant or animal naturally lives and thrives.

4. Narrate — To tell the story in great detail; the voice you hear while the show is playing.

5. Time-lapse — Using pictures shown very quickly to make something like a flower blooming appear sped up.

6. Species — A way of grouping similar kinds of animals or plants scientifically.

7. Schedule — A list of what a person plans to do over a certain period of time.

8. Globe — Another name for our planet Earth.

INSPIRED INNER GENIUS

Muse Museum

More 11G muses to come...

David Attenborough

Sir David Frederick Attenborough was born in 1926 just outside of London, England. He was the second of three boys and he loved learning about natural sciences from an early age. After graduating from high school, he attended Cambridge University and then served for two years in the Royal Navy.

In 1950 he began his career at the BBC, first completing a training program, and then working as a producer. The first educational show he introduced was "Zoo Quest"— it was a big success, setting the groundwork for future nature documentaries to follow. In 1957, the BBC established its Natural History Unit as a response to the success of the show. David also married his wife Jane in 1950 and they had two children, Robert and Susan.

David left the BBC in the 1960s to continue his education and then returned as the controller for BBC 2. Under his leadership the station saw great success, with many shows launched including comedy "Monty Python's Flying Circus". He won many awards for his work during this time.

However, David wanted to focus more on nature documentaries, so he left the BBC in 1972 to work as a freelancer. It was during this time that the "Life" series was first launched, soon followed by Blue Planet and numerous other series highlighting the incredible plants and animals on our planet. In addition to producing and narrating shows, David also wrote many books advocating for the care of the planet as well as several biographies.

David was knighted in 1985 and has received numerous other awards and honorary degrees for the work he has done to preserve the planet and educate millions about all the species that live on it with us.

Sir David Attenborough opens the Turner and the Thames, Five paintings at the artists house in Twickenham on January 10, 2020 in London, England.

GRAB YOUR FREE EDUCATIONAL GUIDE!

This curated guide is the perfect educational tool to center a class around, to bring up at the dinner table, or even to spark an enriching conversation just before bedtime. Scan the QR code or visit us at go.inspiredinnergenius.com/eg to obtain yours!

INSPIRED INNER GENIUS
WHERE GENIUSES CLASH

Here at Inspired Inner Genius, we believe that every child is born a genius.
Join us in our journey to inspire the world, one child at a time.

No part of this publication may be reproduced, stored in a retrieval system, or transmitted, in any form, or by any means, electrical, mechanical, photocopying, recording or otherwise without the prior written permission of the publisher or a licence permitting restricted copying.

Photographic acknowledgement (page 33) Sir David Attenborough opens the Turner and the Thames, Five paintings at the artists house in Twickenham on January 10, 2020 in London, England.
© Photo by Tim P. Whitby via Getty Images

Cover designed by Irina Katsimon · Interior designed by Ana Solarte ·
Written by Abigail Rosas · Published by Inspired Inner Genius